Introduction

Practise your Tenses is a workbook in the *Practise your ...* series which is designed to give students practice in particular areas of English. The main features are these:

- Practice is **contextualised** to make it easier to see the meanings which determine the choice of a particular form.
- Practice is **varied**. There is a mix of exercise types. There is also a mix of exercises focussing on form alone with exercises on the factors which *lie behind* the use of one form rather than another.
- As far as logical grouping of the content allows, practice is **graded** from straightforward practice with easily-stated rules, to language uses which are more complex and require more subtle generalisations.

The material is designed to be suitable both for students working on their own or for classroom use. A few exercises of a more open-ended nature are included to allow students to personalise the language studied. For these it will be helpful to consult a teacher, or other students. But the material does not need a teacher to be present all the time. Many students will find sufficient guidance in the explanations and tables before the exercises, and the possibilities set out by the Answer Key.

The workbook sets out to cover the areas of the tense system which are most important for the learner, briefly, and without too much complication. There are bound to be omissions, but these are either not considered central to tense at this level, or else are covered in other workbooks in the series. For example, the present workbook does not set out to cover tense in a wide range of modal or tag forms, since these areas are dealt with elsewhere. Similarly, the passive is not dealt with as a topic, though some passives are included in the form of *be* with past participle.

The explanations of tenses give some hints on the use of contracted ('short') and uncontracted ('long') forms. In general, the policy has been to give contracted forms – which are used mainly in conversation and informal writing – as the main forms, since they are likely to be of more general use to the learner.

The workbook is intended for adults and young adults, at levels from lower-intermediate to intermediate. It can be used on its own, or as supplementary material to any structural or notional syllabus. It is hoped that the content of the workbook will be found enjoyable as well as useful. The author and the publishers welcome comments from users.

1 Simple present: positive statements and questions

The simple present is used to describe habits and routines, a series of happenings (as in a football commentary), and opinions and feelings.

I You We They	eat wash hurry play do have *etc.*

He She It	eats washes hurries plays does has *etc.*

Do	I you we they	eat? wash? hurry? play? do? have? *etc.*

Does	he she it	eat? wash? hurry? play? do? have? *etc.*

1 Madame Clara is a magician. She is assisted on stage by her husband, Henri. Today she is telling a theatre manager about her act. Fill in the sentences below using the verbs given for each picture. Note that the verbs are not in the correct order.

begin   fly   grow   say

I usually ¹ __begin__ the act

myself. I ² _____ some magic words. A bird

³ _____ out of an empty cage, and a flower

⁴ _____ in an empty pot.

join   put   come   go

Then Henri ⁵ _____ me on the stage. He

⁶ _____ into a box. I ⁷ _____ knives

through the box, but he always ⁸ _____ out

alive!

choose   cover   turn   applaud   tell

Someone from the audience ⁹ _____

a card. I ¹⁰ _____ my back, and Henri

¹¹ _____ my eyes. I ¹² _____

the person what the card is. Everyone in the

audience ¹³ _____ !

catch   disappear   throw

Henri and I ¹⁴ _____ coloured balls

into the audience. But no one ever

¹⁵ _____ them! They

¹⁶ _____ in clouds of smoke!

weigh   try   rise   clap

A strong man from the audience <u>17</u> to lift a piano. He cannot, for it <u>18</u> 1,000 kilos. But I <u>19</u> my hands, and the piano <u>20</u> into the air!

finish   play   hide   vanish   flash

Our act <u>21</u> with a marvellous spectacle. A green light <u>22</u> and the orchestra <u>23</u> a mysterious tune. Then a grey mist <u>24</u> us, and we <u>25</u> like ghosts!

2 The theatre manager is very interested in the act, and he wants to find out everything about it. Write down the questions he asks, using the words given below.

1 How/the bird/fly/out of the cage?
   <u>**How does the bird fly out of the cage?**</u>

2 How/Henri/escape/from the box?
   _____

3 How/the balls/disappear?
   _____

4 How/the piano/rise/into the air?
   _____

5 How/you/do/the trick with the cards?
   _____

6 How/you/make/the grey mist?
   _____

7 How/you and Henri/vanish/at the end?
   _____

8 How long/your act/last?
   _____

5

2 Simple present: mixed positive and negative statements and questions

Don't	I you we they	eat? wash? hurry? *etc.*
Doesn't	he she it	

I You We They	don't do not	eat wash hurry *etc.*
He She It	doesn't does not	

Negative questions with *Why...?* can ask for information **or** make suggestions:

> *Why **don't you like** her?* (asks for information)
> *Why **don't you come** and see us?* (makes a suggestion)

1 The teachers at the Express School of English are having a staff meeting. They are discussing some everyday problems of classes and students. Complete the sentences as in the examples. Use the verbs in brackets, in the negative form where necessary.

JOHN: Abdullah (¹do) _____doesn't do_____ all the written work.

ANNA: Why ² _____doesn't he do it_____ ?

JOHN: Because he only (³need) _____needs_____ spoken English in his job.

MARY: I (⁴use) _____ the computer with my group.

STEVE: Why ⁵_____ ?

MARY: Because the programmes for it (⁶seem) _____ very useful.

SUE: Lucia and Leif (⁷find) _____ the work interesting.

DIRECTOR: Why ⁸_____ ?

SUE: They (⁹think) _____ the level is too low for them.

GARETH: Gustav and I (¹⁰get on) _____ well.

LUCINDA: Oh? Why ¹¹_____ ?

GARETH: The problem is, we (¹²share) _____ the same political opinions.

STEVE: Fatma (¹³come) _____ to the class before lunch on Friday mornings.

JOHN: Why ¹⁴_____ ?

STEVE: Because she (¹⁵go) _____ to the mosque then.

ANNA: The reading textbook (¹⁶suit) _____ the students in my group.

DIRECTOR: Why ¹⁷_____ ?

ANNA: It (¹⁸give) _____ them the kind of practice they need.

LUCINDA: Julio and Sergio (¹⁹like) _____ each other.

MARY: Why ²⁰_____ ?

LUCINDA: Oh, it's because they (²¹disagree) _____ about almost everything.

2 Fill in the blanks in the conversation below, using the correct form of the words given in brackets.

TOM: I (¹hate) _____*hate*_____ spending the whole of the weekend at home. Let's go out.

LUCY: Where (²you want) _____ to go?

TOM: Why (³not we go) _____ to the film club? Most weekends it (⁴show) _____ good films.

LUCY: I (⁵not feel) _____ like seeing a film tonight. But look – the newspaper (⁶say) _____ that Abe Clampit, the jazz pianist, is giving a concert tonight. I (⁷know) _____ you (⁸like) _____ jazz. Why (⁹not we go) _____ to that?

TOM: To be honest, his playing (¹⁰not appeal) _____ to me much.

LUCY: Well, why (¹¹not you go) _____ to the film on your own? It (¹²not matter) _____ to me if I (¹³stay) _____ at home and watch TV for once.

TOM: We could go and see your sister, if you (¹⁴like) _____ . We haven't seen her for ages.

LUCY: That's a good idea. She's lonely where she (¹⁵live) _____ now. She (¹⁶stay) _____ at home all the time. The buses (¹⁷not go) _____ to that part of town, and she (¹⁸not get out) _____ at all.

3 Make suggestions to your partner using the forms:
Why don't we … ? or *Why don't you … ?*
Give a reason for your suggestion.
Your partner agrees or disagrees with the suggestion, and gives a reason.

3 Present progressive: positive and negative statements

The present progressive is used to talk about events which are taking place at the moment of speaking. (For the use of the present progressive to talk about the future, see page 43.)

I'm	reading
You're	lying
We're	making
They're	hitting
He's	hurrying
She's	*etc.*
It's	

In formal, especially formal written language, long forms are used:
I am, you are, we are, they are, he is, she is, it is.

I'm not		reading *etc.*
You We They	aren't	
He She It	isn't	

In formal language, the long forms *I am not, you are not,* etc. are used.

I'm not (reading, etc.*)* is the only short form that can be used with *I.* We can also use this type of short form with other persons: *you're not reading, he's not reading,* etc. This emphasises *not* and makes the negative idea stronger.

> I'm a director at Merlin Books. One of our books has just sold a million copies, so some of us are having a party, and others are just relaxing.

1

Complete the sentences below using the words in brackets. Use negative forms where necessary.

Doris the secretary
(*type, dance*)

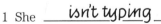

1 She ___isn't typing___ letters. ___She's dancing___ on the table.

Harry the doorman
(*sleep, stand*)

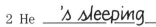

2 He ___'s sleeping___ in a chair. _____ beside the door, today.

Dave and Len, the repair men
(*repair, listen*)

3 They _____ machines. _____ to
the radio.

The company cat
(*sit, catch*)

4 It _____ on the wall. _____
mice, today.

The switchboard operator
(*answer, let*)

5 She *'s not answering* _____ the telephone today. *She's letting* _____ the
answering machine give a recorded message.

The telex machine
(*print, get*)

6 It *'s not printing* _____ messages. *It's getting* _____ dusty.

The directors
(*cut, make*)

7 They *'re cutting* _____ slices of cake. *They're not making* _____ any
important decisions, today.

I
(*eat, try*)

8 But I *'m not eating* _____ anything. *I'm trying* _____ to lose weight.

9

4 Present progressive: positive and negative questions with answers

Am	I	coming? *etc.*
Are	you we they	
Is	he she it	

Aren't	I you we they	coming? *etc.*
Isn't	he she it	

In formal language, or to change the emphasis, the long forms can be used:

> *Why* **am I not** *coming?*,   **Are they not** *coming?*,   etc.

Negative questions beginning with *aren't* and *isn't* (yes/no questions) sometimes suggest surprise or annoyance.

1 Ron Crabb is a youth leader. He is helping to organise a summer camp for some young people. Write questions and answers using the words in the speech bubbles. Use negative forms (with *aren't*, etc.) where necessary.

1 you stand
2 you help
3 do
4 Susie do

'Charlie! Why ¹_____ *are you standing* _____ there doing nothing?

Why ²_____ *aren't you helping* _____ Jill and Tommy in the camp kitchen?'

'Jill and Tommy ³_____ *aren't doing* _____ the cooking today, Ron. It isn't their turn.

⁴_____ the cooking, and she told me she didn't need any help.'

5 Terry take
6 he take
7 he take
8 they use

'Where ⁵_____ these pieces of wood?

Why ⁶_____ them to the campfire?'

'It's OK, Ron. ⁷_____ them to Kim and Mary, on the other side of the camp.

⁸_____ them to build a fence.'

9 you fry
10 they burn
11 I make

'⁹_____ these potatoes too long, Susie?

There's a terrible smell – ¹⁰_____ ?'

'Oh dear, I'm sorry, Ron. ¹¹_____ a real mess of this cooking, aren't I?'

12 I do
13 I lie
14 you help

'What a mess this place is! What ¹²_____ here?

Why ¹³_____ on a beach in Spain – or anywhere except here?!'

'It's your kind heart, Ron! ¹⁴_____ us because you like us so much!'

5 Mixed present simple and progressive forms

1 Marja and Bertrand are students in a language school. They are just getting to know each other. Read part of their conversation. Write the correct form of the verbs in italics (simple or progressive, positive or negative, question or statement). If the verb is already correct, write 'no change'.

BERTRAND: And where ¹*you come from* in Finland, Marja?

MARJA: ²*I come from* Helsinki. But ³*I live* there any more. ⁴*My company, Finn-Sport has* an office in Tempere, so I've moved there.

BERTRAND: I've heard of Finn-Sport. ⁵*They make* skiing equipment?

MARJA: That's right – in fact, all kind of sports equipment. Actually, the company ⁶*pays* for me to study here.

BERTRAND: Really? You're lucky. ⁷*My company sends* anyone on language courses. ⁸*I pay* for this course out of my own pocket.

MARJA: What course ⁹*you take* here? Business English?

BERTRAND: No, ¹⁰*I do* Business English yet. ¹¹*I try* to improve my general English – especially conversation.

MARJA: Well, ¹²*there seems* to be anything wrong with your conversation.

BERTRAND: ¹³*I improve.* By the way, ¹⁴*you know* about the disco ¹⁵*the school organises?*

MARJA: No. When is it?

BERTRAND: Tonight at 9 o'clock. It's at The Magnet Club, in Holland Road.

MARJA: Unfortunately, ¹⁶*I know* where that is.

BERTRAND: It's near where ¹⁷*I live.* Look, why ¹⁸*we meet* before the disco somewhere and have dinner? Then we can go to the disco together.

1 _____*do you come from*_____   10 _____

2 _____   11 _____

3 _____   12 _____

4 _____   13 _____

5 _____   14 _____

6 _____   15 _____

7 _____   16 _____

8 _____   17 _____

9 _____   18 _____

2 Karen is a journalist for a music magazine. She is interviewing Rob Meldon, a singer who sometimes gives free concerts to get money for hungry people. Underline the correct verb phrases in the dialogue below.

KAREN: Rob, ¹*you do/you're doing/are you doing* a lot of work to help hungry people at the moment. What ²*does make/makes/is making* you so interested in helping them?

ROB: Well, ³*I don't read/I'm reading/I read* the newspapers like everyone else. Every week ⁴*you see/do you see/you're seeing* pictures of places where the people ⁵*don't die/do they die/are dying* of hunger. It ⁶*doesn't make/isn't making/makes* me so angry when I see that! ⁷*Isn't it making/Doesn't it make/Does it make* **you** angry?

KAREN: Oh yes, Rob. But a lot of people ⁸*are feeling/feel/do they feel* that the problem is so big that they can't do anything to help. What ⁹*do you say/don't you say/aren't you saying* to this?

ROB: Just that even the smallest gift ¹⁰*doesn't help/does it help/helps* someone. And also, this: just imagine that you ¹¹*are living/aren't living/don't live* in a place where no rain has fallen for years. Perhaps you ¹²*don't want/want/aren't wanting* to accept help from others, but you know you must because your children ¹³*suffer/are suffering/don't suffer.* If your neighbour has food, you'll accept help from him, won't you?

KAREN: Yes. But I ¹⁴*see/don't see/I'm not seeing* exactly what you mean…

ROB: What ¹⁵*I say/I'm saying/I'm not saying* is this: we're all neighbours on this planet, and we can all help. We ¹⁶*aren't needing/need/don't need* to be a special kind of person to do something for others. I mean, ¹⁷*am I looking/do I look/aren't I looking* special? I'm just an ordinary person, and ¹⁸*I help/am I helping/I don't help* in my own way. Anyone can do that.

6 Simple past: positive statements and questions

The simple past is the usual form for talking about events in the past.

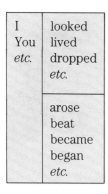

I You etc.	looked lived dropped etc.
	arose beat became began etc.

The simple past form of the verb is the same for all persons. With regular verbs, it ends in -ed.

There are over 250 irregular verbs in English. There is no simple rule for their past forms, but see the list of irregular verbs on page 61.

Did	I you he etc.	look? live? beat? become? begin? etc.

When *did* is used to form questions, the base form of the verb is used for each person. This applies to both regular and irregular verbs.

1 Write the correct past forms in the newspaper reports below. Use the verbs in brackets.

Report 1

Ten-year-old Ann Burns ([1]swim) __*swam*__ over 40 metres yesterday to rescue her younger

brother when he ([2]fall) _____ from a boat in Poole harbour. She

([3]catch) _____ the exhausted boy by the hair and ([4]bring) _____ him safely

to the shore. Then, finding that he was unconscious, she ([5]revive) _____ him by giving

him the 'kiss of life'.

Report 2

Dell United ([6]win) _____ their match against Lee Rovers 3–0 last night, and in so doing

([7]teach) _____ Lee a lesson in the art of football. Lee ([8]find) _____ no

answer to the skill of Dell, who ([9]thrust) _____ forward from the moment the whistle

([10]blow) _____ . Lee ([11]hold on) _____ till half time, but in the 47th minute

Smith, the Dell striker, ([12]shoot) _____ from 50 yards to score a fine goal. Smith ([13]go

on) _____ to score two more goals, and was chosen as man of the match.

Report 3

Police who (^{14}stop) _____ a speeding car yesterday after a ten-mile chase

(^{15}discover) _____ that the driver was Mr A Phelps of Newcastle, aged 103. Mr Phelps

(^{16}learn) _____ to drive in 1906. 'I (^{17}see) _____ the car in my mirror',

(^{18}say) _____ Mr Phelps, but I (^{19}have) _____ no idea it was the police. I

(^{20}put) _____ my foot down and (^{21}drive) _____ off quickly down the

motorway because I (^{22}think) _____ the other car was too close behind me.'

Report 4

During yesterday's severe storms, lightning (^{23}strike) _____ an office building in the

centre of York. It (^{24}start) _____ a fire which (^{25}destroy) _____ the upper

floor of the building and (^{26}cause) _____ £200,000 worth of damage. It

(^{27}take) _____ firemen over four hours to put out the fire.

2 The news editor got the newspaper reports by telephone.
However, the telephone line was very bad. She did not hear a lot
of phrases and had to ask for the information to be repeated.
Write questions which the editor asked, as in the example.

1 When she did not hear *40 metres* (after verb 1) she asked:

   How far did she swim ?

2 When she did not hear *to the shore* (after verb 4) she asked:

_____

3 When she did not hear *by giving him the 'kiss of life'* (after verb 5) she asked:

_____

4 When she did not hear *till half time* (after verb 11) she asked:

_____

5 When she did not hear *in 1906* (after verb 16) she asked:

_____

6 When she did not hear *in my mirror* (after verb 17) she asked:

_____

7 When she did not hear *an office building* (after verb 23) she asked:

_____

8 When she did not hear *£200,000 worth of damage* (after verb 26) she asked:

_____

9 When she did not hear *over four hours* (after verb 27) she asked:

_____

7 Simple past: negative questions and statements

I You etc.	didn't	work eat etc.

Didn't and the base form of the verb are the same for all persons. *Didn't* occurs as *did not* in formal language.

Didn't	I you etc.	work? eat? etc.

Questions beginning with *Didn't...?* often express surprise that something expected may not have happened.

1 Ann is talking to Dick about various things, including her recent holiday abroad. There were some surprises in it. Choose the correct negative forms in the conversation below. Then put a full stop (**.**) or a question mark (**?**) in the boxes, as appropriate.

ANN: $\left\{\begin{array}{l}\text{The plane didn't} \\ \text{Didn't the plane}\end{array}\right\}$ leave until 11.30 – four hours late $\boxed{\cdot}$

DICK: $\left\{\begin{array}{l}\text{They didn't} \\ \text{Didn't they}\end{array}\right\}$ say why it was late $\boxed{}$

ANN: No, they didn't. And then someone was supposed to meet us. But $\left\{\begin{array}{l}\text{he didn't} \\ \text{didn't he}\end{array}\right\}$ arrive $\boxed{}$ Or perhaps he'd come earlier and gone away again.

DICK: Perhaps $\left\{\begin{array}{l}\text{he didn't} \\ \text{didn't he}\end{array}\right\}$ know about the plane being late $\boxed{}$

ANN: Maybe. Anyway, when we finally got to the hotel, $\left\{\begin{array}{l}\text{the hotel didn't} \\ \text{didn't the hotel}\end{array}\right\}$ want to give us rooms $\boxed{}$ $\left\{\begin{array}{l}\text{Didn't they} \\ \text{They didn't}\end{array}\right\}$ have a record of our reservation $\boxed{}$

DICK: $\left\{\begin{array}{l}\text{The travel company didn't} \\ \text{Didn't the travel company}\end{array}\right\}$ send the hotel a list of names $\boxed{}$

ANN: Apparently not. Still, they let us stay in the end.

DICK: From what you say, it sounds as if $\left\{\begin{array}{l}\text{your holiday didn't} \\ \text{didn't your holiday}\end{array}\right\}$ go very well $\boxed{}$

ANN: Well, a lot of things happened that $\left\{\begin{array}{l}\text{didn't I} \\ \text{I didn't}\end{array}\right\}$ expect $\boxed{}$

8 Simple past: mixed forms (positive and negative statements/questions)

1 A group of hill-walkers has arrived back at a youth hostel after getting into difficulties on the hills. The warden of the hostel is finding out what went wrong.
Write the correct form of the verbs in italics (statement or question, positive or negative). If the verb is already correct, write 'no change'.

WARDEN: Ah, there you are! I suppose [1]*you got lost* in the mist!

KEN: No. [2]*The mist covered* our side of the hill.

WARDEN: Well, what happened? Why [3]*you got back* here before now? It [4]*got dark* two hours ago. It was a short trip. [5]*You had to* walk more than eight kilometres.

TOMMY: The problem was that [6]*we took* a map with us …

WARDEN: What! [7]*You took* a map! Why [8]*you checked* that before [9]*you left* this morning?

LIZ: Actually, [10]*we had* a map. But it was the wrong one.

WARDEN: But even without a map, [11]*you have* any idea where you were going? It's just a matter of walking south along the valley. That's all [12]*you needed* to do. [13]*You took* a compass with you?

LARRY: Yes, [14]*Sebastian put* a compass in his pocket this morning. But [15]*he knew* how to use it.

WARDEN: And where is Sebastian now?

KEN: We don't know. [16]*We left* him behind on the hill while he was trying to use his compass.

1 *no change*	9
2	10
3	11
4	12
5	13
6	14
7	15
8	16

9 Past progressive: positive and negative statements/questions

The past progressive is used to make it clear that an action went on **continuously** during, or before and after, or until stopped by a certain event. Note that this 'event' can be another action (e.g. *I was reading when **you telephoned***) or a time (e.g. *I was reading until **12 o'clock** last night*).

I He She It	was	reading lying *etc.*
We You They	were	

I He She It	wasn't was not *(formal)*	reading lying *etc.*
We You They	weren't were not *(formal)*	

Was	I he she it	reading? lying? *etc.*
Were	you they	

Wasn't	I he she it	reading? lying? *etc.*
Weren't	you they	

1 Jill and George have been watching a cowboy film in a foreign language. They are not sure what was happening in it. Now they are discussing the film. Complete the conversation using the words in brackets.

JILL: In the desert scene, I thought ([1]the girl try)

the girl was trying _____ to escape from the

cowboy.

GEORGE: No, ([2]she not try) _____ to

escape from him. ([3]They ride)

_____ off together to escape

from the baddies.

JILL: I don't think so. I'm sure ([4]he chase)

_____ her.

GEORGE: What (⁵they do) _____ in
that scene on the cliff? (⁶They climb)

_____ up the cliff to

surprise the bandits?

JILL: Surely not. (⁷not they climb)

_____ down into the old

mine to find the gold?

JILL: Those men in the bar (⁸make)

_____ plans to rob the

bank, weren't they?

GEORGE: Yes. But one of them (⁹work)

_____ for the sheriff all the

time.

JILL: Oh no! (¹⁰He not work) _____

for the sheriff. (¹¹He plan)

_____ to take all the

money himself!

GEORGE: In the final shoot-out, why (¹²not he aim)

_____ at the leader of the

bandits? Did you notice that? (¹³He shoot)

_____ above his head.

JILL: That's right. (¹⁴He hope)

_____ to capture the

leader alive and find out where the girl was.

JILL: I'm afraid (¹⁵I not watch)

_____ the film all the time.

GEORGE: Why (¹⁶not you watch) _____

it? I thought it was rather fun.

JILL: Oh George, (¹⁷you not watch)

_____ it all the time,

either! In fact (¹⁸you snore) _____

in the middle of it!

10 Past progressive and simple past

1 Here you can see some incidents which took place near Dell football ground last week. A policeman is writing a report of the incidents.

Write sentences from the report, joining ideas together, and using the words given. Sometimes there is more than one possible answer, but BE CAREFUL – in **one** sentence, the past progressive is **not possible with either verb**.

Dell fans enter the ground.

A group of Lee fans arrive.

1 (*while*) <u>While Dell fans were entering the ground, a group of Lee fans arrived</u>.

Several of our men receive injuries.   We try to keep the groups of fans apart.

2 (*while*) _____

We hold our ground well.   A group of Dell fans break through our lines.

3 (*until*) _____
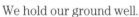

The two groups meet.   Violent fighting breaks out.

4 (*when*) _____

I attempt to arrest one hooligan.

A brick strikes me on the head.

5 (*while*) _____

Several shopkeepers complain to us.

The fans cause a lot of damage.

6 (*because*) _____

All this goes on outside.

Fans throw stones inside the ground.

7 (*while*) _____

The situation becomes serious.   We radio for extra men.

8 (*so*) _____

We wait for extra men.   The situation becomes calm.

9 (*while*) However, _____

21

11 Present perfect: questions and statements; some expressions of frequency

The present perfect is used to talk about actions or events in the past that are still going on in the present, or are still important for the present, or are part of the general experience of someone who is still alive. (It is NOT used when talking about a particular time in the past. Then, the simple past is used.)

I/We/You/They	've have *(formal)*	arrived fallen *etc.*
He/She/It	's has *(formal)*	

Have	I/we/you/they	arrived? fallen? *etc.*
Has	he/she/it	

Position of expressions of frequency:

Have you **ever** *done it?*
No, I've **never** *done it.*
Yes, I've **often** *done it.*
         sometimes

Yes, I've done it once.
            twice.
            several times.
            etc.

1 Look at this table of things Marie Leblanc and her brother Pierre have done, or have not done. Then complete the questions and answers according to the instructions. Use the present perfect tense, and the words in the table.

	ridden a horse	sung in public	wanted to live in America	forgotten their father's birthday	been to England	met *you*	liked the same record
MARIE	never	often	never	once or twice	three times	several times	never
PIERRE	a few times	never	always		never	never	

1 (*Ask Marie about her experience of horse-riding.*) Marie,

have you ever ridden a horse?

(*Give her answer.*) Me? Oh no, _____ .

2 (*Ask Pierre about his experience of horse-riding.*) Pierre,

_____ ?

(*Give his answer.*) Yes, _____ .

3 (*Ask Pierre about Marie's experience of singing in public.*)

Pierre, _____ ?

(*Give Pierre's answer.*) Yes, _____

_____ .

4 (*You want to know Marie's ideas about living in America.*
Ask her.) Marie, _____

_____ ?

(*Give her answer.*) No, _____

_____ .

5 (*You want to know Pierre's ideas about living in America.*
But you are too shy to ask Pierre. Ask Marie instead.) Marie,

_____ ?

(*Give Marie's answer.*) Yes, _____

_____ .

6 (*Are Pierre and Marie good at remembering their father's*
birthday? Ask their father.)

Monsieur Leblanc, _____

_____ ?

(*Give their father's answer.*) _____

_____ .

7 (*Ask Marie about her visits to England.*) Marie, _____

_____ ?

(*Give her answer.*) Yes, _____

_____ .

8 (*You meet Marie at a party. You are not sure if it is your*
first meeting. Ask her a suitable question.) Marie, _____

_____ before?

(*Give Marie's answer.*) Yes, _____

_____ .

9 (*Ask Marie a similar question about meeting* Pierre *before.*)

_____

_____ ?

(*Give Marie's answer.*) _____

_____ .

12 Present perfect: positive and negative forms; use with *for* and *since*

Present perfect negative

I/we/you/they	haven't have not *(formal)*	arrived come *etc.*
He/she/it	hasn't has not *(formal)*	

Notes on *for* and *since*:

*I have been here **for** two hours.*
  (= period of time up to the present)
*I have**n't** played tennis **for** ten years.*
  (= period of time up to the present)
*I have been here **since** eight o'clock.*
  (= point of time in the past)

1 Members of the Staywell Keep-Fit Club gave up a lot of bad habits some years ago and started to live in a very healthy way. The president of the club is talking about some of the members. Make sentences using the present perfect with *for* or *since*, according to the sentences and words given. Use positive or negative forms as indicated.

1 Sid stopped smoking 18 years ago. (*smoke* (negative), *for*)
  Sid hasn't smoked for 18 years.

2 Don became a vegetarian in 1980. (*be* (positive), *since*)
  _____

3 Liza began to be interested in healthy eating five years ago. (*be* (positive), *for*)
  _____

4 Sam gave up alcohol after his car accident. (*drink* (negative), *since*)
  _____

5 I started running two kilometres every morning in 1985. (*run* (positive), *since*)
  _____

6 Mary stopped going to bed after midnight two years ago. (*stay up* (negative), *for*)
  _____

7 Sue and Pam stopped taking useless medicines when they joined the health club.
  (*take* (negative), *since*)
  _____

8 Bob and I play squash every Friday night. This began when the squash court opened.
  (*play* (positive), *since*)
  _____

13 Present perfect: mixed simple forms, including negative questions

Haven't	I/we/you/they	come?
Hasn't	he/she/it	etc.

Examples:
Haven't they arrived yet?
Why **haven't you told** them about it?
Why **hasn't she paid** the money?

1 Mr Barker has arrived at the office in a bad mood. Write the correct form of the verbs in italics (question or statement, positive or negative). If the verb is already correct, write 'no change'.

BARKER: I asked for the payments list yesterday. It isn't here. Why [1]*it has arrived* on my desk?

NORRIS: The people in the payments office [2]*have been* very busy recently. Perhaps [3]*they have had* time to find it for you.

BARKER: Humph! And you, Nora. [4]*I have told* you always to have a cup of coffee waiting for me when I arrive?

NORA: I'm sorry Mr Barker. The coffee machine [5]*has broken down.*

BARKER: Bah! [6]*I have had* any breakfast this morning, and now you tell me there's no coffee! And look! [7]*The cleaner has emptied* my ashtray. It's still full of cigarette ends from yesterday.

DAVE: (whispers to Nora): What a bad mood he's in! Perhaps [8]*his wife has gone* on a business trip again.

NORA: (whispers to Dave): Or perhaps [9]*she has told* him how wonderful he is. [10]*He's always liked* hearing that kind of thing, you know.

NORRIS: Er ... Mr Barker, [11]*you have forgotten* something this morning?

BARKER: What is it now?

NORRIS: [12]*I've arranged* your meeting with Mr Nashimuro, the head of Tony Electronics, just as you asked me to do yesterday. But [13]*you have put* your tie on.

BARKER: Oh dear no, you're right. [14]*I've forgotten* my tie. Can I borrow yours?

1 _____ *hasn't it arrived* ? _____

2 _____

3 _____

4 _____

5 _____

6 _____

7 _____

8 _____

9 _____

10 _____

11 _____

12 _____

13 _____

14 _____

14 Present perfect progressive: questions and statements; negative statements

The present perfect progressive is used to describe **continuous** or **repeated** actions extending from the past into the present (or almost to the present). Questions using the present perfect continuous may be understood as complaints or accusations:

*Who's **been borrowing** books without permission?.*

I/We/You/They	've have (*formal*)	been	dreaming *etc.*
He/She/It	's has (*formal*)		

Have	I/we/you/they	been	dreaming? *etc.*
Has	he/she/it		

I/We/You/They	haven't have not (*formal*)	been	dreaming *etc.*
He/She/It	hasn't has not (*formal*)		

Negative questions (e.g. *Haven't I been telling you... ?, Why hasn't he been working?*) are not so common, and are not practised below.

1 Several students live together in a flat. Gina is in charge of buying the food. Read her conversation with Kate. Make the correct present perfect progressive form from the words in brackets.

GINA: Kate, (¹I look) ___*I've been looking*___ in the fridge. It looks as if (²someone use) _____ a lot of food. Is it you, Kate? (³you do) _____ a lot of cooking?

KATE: No. (⁴I not use) _____ the kitchen much. (⁵I eat) _____ at the student cafeteria.

GINA: Well, what about Vera and Julie? (⁶they entertain) _____ their friends here? I'm sure I've heard them talking to friends late at night.

KATE: Well, I think (⁷Vera discuss) _____ politics with her friends during the student elections. But I'm almost sure (⁸she not cook) _____ . You know how she hates cooking. And as for Julie, (⁹she stay) _____ out late with her friends most nights.

GINA: Anyway, (¹⁰we spend) _____ a lot of money on food recently.

KATE: Well, it isn't surprising, is it? (¹¹Prices go up) _____ all the time.

15 Present perfect: mixed simple and progressive forms

1 Mrs Ellis is writing to her son, Thomas, who is a student. Write the most suitable present perfect form (simple or progressive) using the words in brackets.

Dear Thomas,

(¹ It be) _____It has been_____ several weeks since we last had a letter from you. (² We hope) _____ to hear from you. Why (³ not you write) _____ to us? You know how much your letters (⁴ always mean) _____ to us.

(⁵ I send)_____ a parcel to you with some food and warm clothes. Your father (⁶ save) _____ the weekly sports magazines you like to read, and (⁷ we put) _____ these in the parcel too.

Life (⁸ go on) _____ as usual here. Mr Jones next door, who (⁹ not enjoy) _____ good health recently, (¹⁰ have to) _____ go into hospital. (¹¹ He have) _____ an operation and will be home again soon. Meanwhile, his cat (¹² come) _____ to us for food and milk. I think (¹³ we manage) _____ to look after it quite well.

(¹⁴ you see) _____ anything of Mark Andrews? Apparently (¹⁵ he leave) _____ school now and is at the same college as you. (¹⁶ We get) _____ news of him regularly from his mother. But, of course, he's two years younger than you. (¹⁷ He not say) _____ whether (¹⁸ he meet) _____ you or not.

By now your first exams will be over. We hope (¹⁹ you do) _____ well in them. Do write soon.

Lots of love,
Mum.

16 Present perfect and simple past

1 Complete the passage below, using the correct form of the verb in brackets (present perfect or simple past).

The Olympic Games

The original Olympic Games (¹begin) _____**began**_____ around 800 BC in Ancient Greece, and (²continue) _____ until they (³be) _____ abolished by the Roman Emperor Theodosius in AD 393. The first modern Olympics (⁴take place) _____ in Athens in 1896, and since then, more than a dozen different countries (⁵stage) _____ the Summer Olympics. The cities of Paris, London, Berlin and Los Angeles (⁶stage) _____ the Olympics twice.

In 1956, Australia (⁷become) _____ the first country outside Europe and America to stage the Olympics, while Mexico (⁸be) _____ the first Latin American country to stage the Olympics, in 1968.

Many of the greatest athletes in the world (⁹take part) _____ in the Olympic Games, but no one (¹⁰equal) _____ the achievements of the great Finnish athlete, Paavo Nurmi, who between 1920 and 1928 (¹¹win) _____ nine gold and three silver medals.

The Olympic Games (¹²see) _____ many tragedies and triumphs. For example, in the marathon of 1908, the little Italian, Dorando Pietri (¹³collapse) _____ five times in the last part of the race, but (¹⁴come) _____ first – only to be disqualified because spectators (¹⁵help) _____ him over the finishing line. And in 1936, the famous black American athlete Jesse Owens, (¹⁶break) _____ six world records in a single day!

From the first modern Olympics in Athens, when only fourteen countries (¹⁷participate) _____ , the Olympics (¹⁸grow) _____ to include over 140 countries. Gold, silver and bronze medals (¹⁹go) _____ to over 8,000 men and women.

17 Past perfect: positive and negative statements and questions

The past perfect is used when we look back from a certain time in the past to an even earlier time in the past.

I You He/She We They	had 'd *(informal)*	eaten *etc.*
It had		

Had	I you he/she/it we they	eaten? *etc.*

I You He/She/It We They	hadn't had not *(formal)*	eaten *etc.*

Hadn't you, *etc.* Had you, *etc.* not *(formal)*	eaten? *etc.*

The happiest moment of my life was on top of a mountain in Wales last summer. I was happy for a lot of different reasons …

1 A group of students are remembering happy moments in their lives. Complete what Hugo says, using the past perfect, and the ideas under the pictures.

1 ___ *I had climbed a mountain.* ___

I climb a mountain.

2 _____

The rope doesn't break.

3 _____

My girlfriend agrees to marry me.

29

4 _____

A letter comes with good news about my exams.

5 _____

I spend a wonderful holiday in Wales.

6 _____

My favourite team wins the football championship.

2 If a room is noisy, we often have to ask questions about the information we haven't heard. What can you ask if you don't hear all of the words Hugo says? For example, you may not hear:

1 *climbed the mountain* in sentence 1, so you ask:

　What had you done? _____

2 *the rope* in sentence 2, so you ask:

　What hadn't broken? _____

3 *marry me* in sentence 3, so you ask:

　What _____

4 *good news about my exams* in sentence 4, so you ask:

　What _____

5 *Wales* in sentence 5, so you ask:

　Where _____

6 *football championship* in sentence 6, so you ask:

　What _____

18 Past perfect progressive: positive and negative statements

The past perfect progressive is used when we look back from a certain time in the past to continuous or repeated actions at an even earlier time in the past.

I You He/She/It We They	had 'd *(informal)*	been dreaming *etc.*
It had		

I You He/She/It We They	hadn't had not *(formal)*	been dreaming *etc.*

1

The government of Pacifica started an investigation into its security services after several of its secret agents went over to its enemy, Arctica.
Complete the sentences from the investigator's report, using the verbs in brackets. Use a negative where the meaning of the sentence requires it.

What went wrong? Our investigation revealed the following facts:

1 'Some of our agents (work) ___*had been working*___ for the enemy for several years.'

2 'We (give away) _____ secrets to the enemy over a long period.'

3 'The departments in our security services (cooperate) _____ well with each other.'

4 'Our most trusted agent in Arctica (have) _____ problems in her marriage.'

5 'The enemy (listen) _____ to conversations between our agents, using secret listening devices.'

6 'Our agents (receive) _____ enough money to carry out their operations.'

7 'We ought to have guessed that something was wrong; over a period of several months we (get) _____ any useful information out of Arctica.'

8 'The enemy (feed) _____ us false information.'

9 'For several weeks, one of our agents in Arctica (send) _____ , messages in the wrong code. We should have realised that he had been captured.'

10 'The conclusion: our security services (carry out) _____ their duties efficiently.'

19 Past perfect: mixed simple and progressive forms

Positive past perfect progressive questions are formed as follows:
> **Had** I/you/she (etc.) **been dreaming?**

Negative questions (e.g. *Hadn't you been expecting this?*) are not so common, and are not practised below.

1 Wendy is telling Jo about some of the difficulties she had on her wedding day. Write the verbs in italics in a suitable past perfect form (positive or negative, simple or progressive). If the verb is already correct, write 'no change'.

WENDY: Well, first of all, I couldn't get my wedding dress to fit. The dressmaker ¹*had made* a mistake in the measurements.

JO: ²*You had tried it on* in the dressmaker's before that?

WENDY: ³*I'd had* a first fitting two weeks before, but ⁴*I had tried on* the final version. There hadn't been time. ⁵*I had made* so many other arrangements for the wedding. Anyway, after my sister ⁶*had altered* the dress with her sewing machine, Dave phoned to say he couldn't go ahead with the wedding. He said he wasn't well. ⁷*He'd been* sick that morning.

JO: ⁸*He had celebrated* the night before?

WENDY: Oh yes. ⁹*He had had* a good time with some of the men from his work. And I suppose with all the excitement ¹⁰*he had slept* well. But I thought he had other reasons. Anyway, I was so angry ... ¹¹*I'd almost decided* to call the whole thing off. But then he phoned again. ¹²*He had talked* to his father ...

JO: ¹³*His father had given* him a few words of fatherly advice?

WENDY: Yes, I suppose that was it. Anyway, ¹⁴*he'd calmed down,* and he wanted to go ahead. And we did. And we've been happy ever since.

1 ___no change___

2 _____

3 _____

4 _____

5 _____

6 _____

7 _____

8 _____

9 _____

10 _____

11 _____

12 _____

13 _____

14 _____

20 Mixed past and perfect forms: statements about the past

1 Complete the newspaper report below using a suitable form of the verbs in brackets. Sometimes more than one answer is possible.

Maria Campos (^{1}become) __*has become*__ a rising

star in the Progressive Party. She (^{2}begin)

_____ her political career while she

(^{3}study) _____ at Woodsville University.

When she first (^{4}stand) _____ as a

candidate for Woodsville, she (^{5}not win)

_____ many votes – Woodsville is a

traditional town, and no woman (^{6}ever be)

_____ a candidate there before. 'They (^{7}elect) _____

the same man, year after year,' she told me, 'and they (^{8}just laugh) _____ at

me when I (^{9}get up) _____ to speak.' But she was the winning candidate in

the next election, and since then she (^{10}show) _____ herself to be a hard-

hitting speaker who (^{11}never be) _____ afraid to say what she thinks.

In recent months she (^{12}fight) _____ hard to improve the position of

women. She told me the reason. 'I began this campaign because women (^{13}continually write)

_____ to me, complaining of how their husbands

(^{14}treat) _____ them. Sometimes their husbands (^{15}throw them out)

_____ of the family home and left them without any possessions. The law

(^{16}always take) _____ the husband's side in such cases.'

When I (^{17}interview) _____ Maria Campos last week, she (^{18}plan)

_____ a new campaign on this question. She (^{19}already persuade) _____

_____ some of the country's most important legal experts to support her. 'The law must

be changed,' she (^{20}tell) _____ me.

33

21 Mixed past and perfect forms: statements and questions about the past

1 What could you say in these situations? Write your own ideas. Use the tense in brackets. Make the verb negative if necessary.

Example:
You go to the doctor because of a problem about sleeping. What do you say? (*present perfect progressive*)

_____ **I've been sleeping badly.** _____

or _____ **I haven't been sleeping well.** _____

1 The police ask you about your activities at the time a crime was committed. Answer the question. (*past progressive*)

I _____ .

2 You are a teacher. You see that the homework you expected from one pupil is missing. What do you ask? (*present perfect*)

Why _____ ?

3 You are surprised that a friend doesn't know what happened at a meeting. Is it possible that she wasn't at the meeting? Ask your friend a question. (*past simple*)

_____ the meeting?

4 Someone asks you your reason for not coming to your team's football practice. Answer the question. (*past simple*)

The reason was that _____ .

5 You are sorry about a friend's recent illness. What do you tell your friend? (*present perfect*)

I'm sorry that _____ .

6 You remember an occasion when you were punished as a child. Say what led up to it. (*past perfect*)

I _____ .

7 Some students are discussing why Pacifica went to war with Arctica fifty years ago. You give your opinion. (*past perfect*)

I think it was because _____

_____

8 A friend tells you that he has passed his driving test. You wonder if this was expected. Ask a question. (*past simple*)

_____ ?

9 You hear that your friend Ann has been in a car accident. You wonder if she was the driver. Ask a question. (*past progressive*)

_____ ?

22 Future with *will* and *shall*

Uses:

1 Promises: *I'**ll** help you.*
2 Predictions: *The population of the world* **will** *reach six billion by 1995.*
3 Decisions at the moment of deciding: *Very well – I'**ll** see him.*
4 Plans, with expressions of possibility or with conditions:
  *Perhaps I'**ll** do it; I think I'**ll** do it; I'**ll** do it if I can.*
5 Offers, suggestions, and requests for advice: **Shall** *I do it for you?* **Shall** *we go now? What* **shall** *I do?*
6 Orders and requests: *You'**ll** do exactly as I tell you;* **Will** *you close that window?*
7 Refusals: *I* **won't/shan't** *do it.*

I'll You'll He'll/She'll/It'll We'll They'll	come *etc.*

In formal language, *'ll* occurs as *will*, except with *I* and *we*, when it occurs as *shall*. (But nowadays, *will* is often used in statements with *I* and *we* also.)

Shall	I we	come? *etc.*
Will	you he/she/it they	

It is safer to use *shall* (not *will*) in questions with *I* and *we*. *Shall I … ?* and *Shall we … ?* are the preferred forms when asking for instructions, suggestions or advice (*What shall I do?* etc.).

I We You He/She/It They	won't	come *etc.*	or	I We	shan't	come *etc.*

In formal language, *won't* occurs as *will not*, and *shan't* occurs as *shall not. Shan't* is rare in American English.

Won't	I you *etc.*	come? *etc.*

1 Promises

A salesman is trying to sell a computer. Complete what he says with *'ll, will* or *won't*.

'This is an excellent machine which ¹_____ **will** _____ give you many years of service. We ²_____ install it for you. We ³_____ even give you a special course to teach you how to use it. But you ⁴_____ find it difficult to learn. You ⁵_____ soon see how easy it is to store information and to type letters with this computer.

Now, about the payment. We ⁶_____ ask you for immediate payment. It
⁷_____ be OK if you make a small payment now, and you can pay the rest in three
months' time – we ⁸_____ send you a letter to remind you. What's more, we
⁹_____ give you a 5% reduction on the marked price. And of course, the computer
¹⁰_____ come to you with a two-year guarantee. But actually, you ¹¹_____
need the guarantee, because there ¹²_____ be any problems with the machine. If there
are, I ¹³_____ deal with them personally.

So you want to buy it? Good! I can tell you, sir, you ¹⁴_____ be sorry! Actually,
I ¹⁵_____ give you this machine here in the showroom – it's a demonstration model, and
it's rather dusty. I ¹⁶_____ get you another one from the store downstairs. Please wait a
moment, sir. I ¹⁷_____ be back in a minute.'

2 Predictions

Write predictions (what **you** think, or what your **neighbour**
thinks). Use *will* or *won't*. Be ready to give **reasons** for the
predictions.

In 100 years' time …

    There won't be as many people as there are now.

or _There will be a lot more people than there are now._

1 Will cars be powered by petrol? Electric batteries? Atomic power?

_____

2 Will people still smoke cigarettes?

_____

3 Will people speak the same language all over the world?

_____

4 Will there be drugs against every kind of disease?

_____

Make a prediction of your own about the world in 100 years' time.

5 _____

How about **you**? In **five** years' time will you speak English better
than you do now? Have the same job as you have now? Be
married? Be rich? Write two predictions about yourself.

6 _____

7 _____

23 Questions with *shall* for offers, suggestions; requests for suggestions and advice

1 Look at this table. Then write questions from the table to match the answers given below:

Shall		I	cook a meal for you?
What Where	shall	we	go to Spain for our holiday this year? do if the money doesn't reach me in time? do the shopping? dance? take Aunt Martha when she comes to visit? wear at the wedding?

1 _____Shall I do the shopping_____ ?

Yes please. I'll stay at home and look after the children.

2 _____ ?

I'd rather stay in England.

3 _____ ?

Later, perhaps. I feel a little tired at the moment.

4 _____ ?

Let's show her the museum and the art gallery.

5 _____ ?

No thanks, I'm not hungry.

6 _____ ?

Go to your bank manager and ask him for a loan.

7 _____ ?

Why don't you buy a new dress?

24 Future with *will* and *shall*: mixed questions and statements

1 The year is 1890, during the Pacifican Civil War. A group of rebels
are expecting an attack by government soldiers.
Look at the verb phrases in italics. Write them with the correct
form of *will* or *shall* (question or statement, positive or negative).
If the verb is already correct, write 'no change'.

LUCAN: Do you think [1]*they'll attack* today, commander?
VARGEZ: My guess is that [2]*they'll attack* until the sun goes down. But [3]*we'll be* ready for them,
         whenever they come.
TAIT: [4]*They'll be* heavily armed, do you think?
VARGEZ: No. They're coming over difficult country, so probably [5]*they'll be* heavily armed.
BELOF: How many of them [6]*there will be*?
VARGEZ: Probably around fifty. Anyway, [7]*there will be* more than 100 of them, at the very most.
LUCAN: If they want to take us by surprise, [8]*they'll come* at night, through Drybones Canyon. [9]*I'll
         go up* to Skull Rock? I can see the canyon clearly from there, even at night.
VARGEZ: OK. But how [10]*you'll let* us know if you see the enemy? Wait … I've got a plan. Lucan –
         [11]*you'll wave* a burning stick when you see them. [12]*We'll take* **them** by surprise, in the
         canyon. [13]*They'll see* us coming. I promise you, men, [14]*we'll let* them get away!
TAIT: But what [15]*we'll do* if they have the new Leafield machine guns?
VARGEZ: [16]*We'll give* them time to get their guns ready. Come on, men! [17]*This will be* a great victory
         for us!

1 ___no change___   7 _____   13 _____

2 _____   8 _____   14 _____

3 _____   9 _____   15 _____

4 _____   10 _____   16 _____

5 _____   11 _____   17 _____

6 _____   12 _____

25 Future with *going to*

Uses:

1 To talk about a future situation which already has signs or causes in the present: *Look at that wall! It's leaning out – it's* **going to fall down** *one of these days.*

2 To talk about intentions concerning things already decided (not newly decided): *I'm* **going to paint** *my room this summer – I've already chosen the colours I want.*

3 To express firm determination: *He said that about me, did he?* *I'm* **going to say** *something to him when I see him next!*

I'm	going to	fall
You're We're They're		*etc.*
He's She's It's		

As usual, the uncontracted forms *I am, you are, he is,* etc. can occur in formal language.

I'm not	going to	fall
You/We/They aren't		*etc.*
He/She/It isn't		

Negatives with *not* can be used with all persons:
You're not going to have this one.
He's not going to get help from me. etc.
This may suggest strong determination **not** to allow something to happen.

Am I	going to	fall?
Are we/you/they		*etc.*
Is he/she/it		

Am I not	going to	fall?
Aren't you/they/we		*etc.*
Isn't he/she/it		

1 *Going to* for future situations with signs observable in the present

Look at the pictures below. What do you think is happening in them? Write questions with *going to* using the words in brackets. Then answer the question according to your own ideas, and give a reason.

Example: (it – rain)

QUESTION: *Is it going to rain?*

ANSWER + REASON: *Yes, it's going to rain. There are clouds in the sky.*
or *No, it isn't going to rain. The clouds are going away.*

1 (monkeys – reach the banana)

_____ ?

_____

_____

2 (they – find the treasure)

_____ ?

_____

_____

3 (she – rescue the man in the water)

_____ ?

_____

_____

4 (building – fall down)

_____ ?

_____

_____

5 (it – get dark)

_____ ?

_____

_____

6 (she – get married)

_____ ?

_____

_____

Now compare your answers with a partner.

2 *Going to* for intentions already decided and firm determination

Read the following situations. Write or complete sentences to match each situation. Use negatives where necessary.

1 Susan has decided to buy a new dress. What does she tell her friend?

   <u>I'm going to buy a new dress.</u>

2 Her friend wants to know more. What does she ask?

   What kind of _____ ?

3 Susan has decided that the dress she needs is an evening dress. How does she answer her friend?

   It _____ .

4 Mr Butcher is a teacher at Rottenbrick School. He is determined to stop some boys from playing football in the playground. What does he tell them?

   _____

   in the playground, do you hear?

5 Later, he sees that someone has written a rude message about him on the blackboard. What does he say to himself?

   _____ the boy who wrote

   this message! _____ let

   him get away with it!

6 Arctica has declared war on Pacifica. The Chief of the Arctican army is getting his soldiers ready to march. What does he say to the soldiers?

   Soldiers! The time has come! Tomorrow _____

   _____ into Pacifica!

7 The soldiers of Arctica do not want to fight. What do they say?

   The people of Pacifica are our brothers. _____

   _____ to fight them!

26 Mixed *will/shall* and *going to* forms

1 John and Carol are making plans for a day's holiday. Form a
suitable *will/shall* or *going to* form from the words in brackets.
Sometimes both forms are possible.

JOHN: Look, there isn't a cloud in the sky. ([1]It be) _____It's going to be_____ a

glorious day. ([2]we go) _____ to the beach?

CAROL: ([3]I go) _____ to the beach, but ([4]I not swim) _____

_____ . The water's still too cold.

JOHN: I don't think ([5]I swim) _____ either. But ([6]I take) _____

_____ my swimming things with me. If the sun gets very hot I expect ([7]I be

glad) _____ to jump into the water.

CAROL: ([8]I lie) _____ in the sun a lot this year. I need sunshine after all

the rain during the winter. I know ([9]it do) _____ me good.

JOHN: It's a holiday today. That means ([10]there be) _____ a big crowd

of people at the seaside.

CAROL: But I'm sure ([11]there not be) _____ too many at Whitesands

Beach. ([12]We probably have) _____ the place almost to

ourselves.

JOHN: What ([13]we do) _____ about lunch? ([14]I make) _____

_____ some sandwiches?

CAROL: It's OK. ([15]I make) _____ them, if you go and get the car ready.

2 In which blanks above are **both** *will/shall* **and** *going to* forms
possible? Give three examples.
Numbers _____ , _____ , _____ .

27 Future expressed by present progressive: contrast with *will* and *going to* future

Uses:

The present progressive (*we're meeting*, etc.) can be used to talk about the future in the following cases:

1 The 'arranged future', for arrangements that have already been made: ***I'm seeing*** *him at 10 o'clock tomorrow – I've already phoned him about it;* ***We're getting*** *a new room added to our house – the work is due to begin next week.*

2 With **any** intention, when there is a verb of motion: ***I'm going*** *to London tomorrow.*

3 In general questions about plans: ***Are you doing*** *anything tonight?*

Read the situations below. In most (not all) of them, you could use a present progressive form, but another form may be possible also. Choose (a), (b) or (c) and circle the letter.

1 Helen's secretary reminds her of her intention to travel to Chicago. What does the secretary say?
   a Remember – you're flying to Chicago next week.
   b Remember – you'll fly to Chicago next week.
   c Either (a) or (b).

2 Jim has invited some friends to his house for dinner. As a result, he cannot go to a football match. What does he say?
   a I can't go. I'm having a meal with friends that night.
   b I can't go. I'll have a meal with friends that night.
   c Either (a) or (b).

3 Terry has to go away for a few days. He is worried about what will happen to his cat during his absence. His neighbour promises to help. What does the neighbour say?
   a Don't worry. I'm feeding it while you're away.
   b Don't worry. I'll feed it while you're away.
   c Either (a) or (b).

4 Andrew has booked a hotel in Athens as part of a business trip. What does he say?
   a I'm spending four nights in Athens.
   b I'm going to spend four nights in Athens.
   c Either (a) or (b).

5 Marion isn't looking forward to the arrival of workmen next week. She knows the house will be in a mess. What does she say to her friend?
   a What a nuisance! We're getting central heating put in next week.
   b What a nuisance! We'll get central heating put in next week.
   c Either (a) or (b).

29 Future progressive with *will + ing*

Uses:

1 For actions or events that occur as a matter of course, with no deliberate intention or effort: ***I'll be seeing*** him at the club tomorrow – *he's usually there when I'm there.*

2 Out of politeness, to avoid any idea of wanting, requesting or promising: ***Will you be going*** *there?* (compare *Will you go there for me?*), *Yes,* ***I'll be going*** *there* (compare *Yes, I'll go there because you've asked me to*).

3 For continuous actions taking place before and after, or during some future time: *At seven o'clock tomorrow* ***I'll be having*** *my breakfast.*

I'll You'll He'll/She'll We'll They'll	be	coming *etc.*
It will		

In formal language, *'ll* occurs as *will*, or as *shall* with *I* and *we* (see page 35).

I You *etc.*	won't be	coming *etc.*

Won't occurs as *will not* in formal language. In British English, *shan't* or *shall not* (formal) can be used with *I* and *we* (see also page 35).

Will	I you *etc.*	be	coming? *etc.*

Positive questions, e.g. ***Will you be seeing*** *him?,* ***You'll be seeing*** *him tonight,* ***won't you?*** are fairly common. Negative questions, e.g. *Won't she be speaking at the meeting?* are heard less often, and are not practised below.

1 The Tibbs family have just come back from a long trip round the world. For most of them, this means that they will go back to their ordinary (rather boring) routines. You are looking at some photographs with Mrs Tibbs, and asking questions about the family's plans now.

Form questions and answers, using the words given.

What (¹Sue do) ___will Sue be doing___ ?

for the rest of this year?

(²she go back) _____ to her

old school?

Yes. (³She play) _____ with
her friends again. (⁴She not ride) _____
_____ on camels in Arabia.

How about Tim and tom? I expect (⁵they camp)
_____ with the Scouts again, won't
they?

Oh yes. (⁶They camp) _____ with
the Scouts. (⁷They not camp) _____
on the plains of Kenya.

And you and your husband? (⁸you have) _____
_____ another holiday this year?

No. (⁹We stay) _____ in Newtown.
(¹⁰We not gaze) _____ at the Taj
Mahal by moonlight!

And you, yourself? (¹¹You come) _____
_____ to the Women's Club this year, won't you?

That's right. (¹²I make) _____ jam
for the Women's Club. (¹³I not make) _____
_____ birds' nest soup unless it comes out of a tin!

How about Grandpa Tibbs? I suppose (¹⁴he have) _____
_____ his daily beer and sausage at the Crown
Hotel, again, won't he?

Of course. (¹⁵He eat) _____ good
old British food. (¹⁶He not eat) _____
snails in Paris.

And what about Grandma Tibbs? (¹⁷she stay) _____
_____ in Newtown?

No, (¹⁸she not come back) _____ to
Newtown for another two years. She's going round the world
again!

30 Future progressive: contrasted with *will* future, *going to* future and present progressive

1 Choose the best answers in the dialogue below. Circle (a), (b) or (c).

MRS FOY: ^1a Will you be doing
      b Are you doing   anything special tomorrow, Bill?
      (*c*) Either (a) or (b).

                           ^2a I'll be going
BILL: Not really. I suppose   *b* I'll go   to Newtown as usual in the morning and in
                           c Either (a) or (b).
               ^3a I'll be studying
    the afternoon   *b* I'll study   for my exams.
               c Either (a) or (b).

      ^4a Will you be getting
MRS FOY: *b* Will you get   something for me from the shops in Newtown, please?
      c Either (a) or (b).

                  ^5a I'll be doing
BILL: Yes, of course. I expect   *b* I'm doing   some of my own shopping anyway.
                    c Either (a) or (b).

MRS FOY: You see, I need a mousetrap. Last night I heard a mouse in the house. I hate
                ^6a I'll be catching
    mice! I've decided   *b* I'm going to catch   it.
                  c Either (a) or (b).

         ^7a I'll be getting
BILL: Well, certainly   *b* I'll get   one for you. But why don't you buy a cat?
            c Either (a) or (b).
^8a I'll be getting ^9a I'll be seeing
   b I'm going to get   one soon. In fact,   *b* I'm seeing   a man
   c Either (a) or (b).   *c* Either (a) or (b).
                   ^{10}a he'll be having
    about it at the weekend. Perhaps   *b* he'll have   a kitten that would suit you, too.
                   c Either (a) or (b).

31 Future perfect: contrasted with future progressive

The future perfect is used to predict situations at certain times in the future. It refers to actions or events that will already be completed at these times.

I'll You'll He'll/She'll/It'll We'll They'll	have	finished *etc.*

In formal language, *will* and *shall* occur in the usual way (see page 35). See page 35 also for the use of *will not, shan't* and *shall not.*

I You *etc.*	won't	have	finished

Will	I you *etc.*	have	finished?

1 The president of Pacifica is making a speech on television. Complete the blanks with a suitable future perfect (*will have done*) or future progressive (*will be doing*) form. Use the words in brackets.

1 Citizens of Pacifica! In twelve months' time, the average income of our people (rise)

will have risen _____ by five per cent, while inflation (not rise) _____

_____ at all.

2 By 1992, neighbouring countries (marvel) _____ at our progress, for

they (not equal) _____ our success.

3 In fact, by 1993, we (overtake) _____ Arctica and Atlantica.

4 By 1994, our factories (produce) _____ all the goods we need.

5 By 1995, the number of schools in our country (double) _____ .

6 By 1996, we (build) _____ 200 new hospitals.

7 By 1997, you (enjoy) _____ a better standard of living than at any

time in our country's history!

28 Future expressed by simple present

The simple present is used for events in the future which are part of a prearranged programme or timetable:

*The meeting **starts** at 6 o'clock.*
*We **leave** on Thursday.*

1

Mrs King, Director of Studies at Brightburgh College, is telling the staff about arrangements for welcoming new students to the college tomorrow.
Complete what she says by using the verbs in the box, in their correct form. Usually, the simple present is suitable, but in THREE blanks the future with *going to* should be used.

| assemble | get | meet | try out | visit | make | return |
| give | divide | arrive | begin | have | finish | enjoy |

So please, everyone, listen carefully. The new students [1] **assemble** tomorrow at 10 o'clock. We [2]_____ them coffee and biscuits, and then at 10.45, Mr Carruthers, the Principal of the College [3]_____ the usual speech of welcome. After that we [4]_____ the students into groups to visit different parts of the building.

As some of you may know, this year we [5]_____ a new examination system, including a special project using books from the college library. So part of the programme tomorrow is that at twelve o'clock the groups [6]_____ in the library for a talk from Mrs Lindsey, the librarian.

Now, as regards tomorrow afternoon: at two o'clock the bus [7]_____ to take students on a tour of Brightburgh. According to the radio, the weather [8]_____ much colder tomorrow, so we should advise students to take a coat with them. During the afternoon we [9]_____ the Roman Camp and the Cathedral, and then around five o'clock the bus [10]_____ to the college.

As far as the evening is concerned, the party for new students [11]_____ at half past seven. We [12]_____ a very nice programme arranged for this, so I know everyone [13]_____ it. The party [14]_____ around half past eleven.

32 Mixed forms expressing the future

1 Danny is a young businessman. He is planning to open a disco –
but he needs more money. He asks another man, Ned Lucas, to
help him with the money.
Fill in the blanks below with a suitable form expressing the future.
Use the words in brackets. Often, more than one answer is
possible.

'Ned, (¹I open) _____ **I'm going to open** _____ a disco. I've been planning this for some

months now. But (²it take) _____ a lot of money to get it started. (³you lend)

_____ me £50,000? (⁴I pay) _____ it back soon – (⁵you not have

to) _____ wait long.

    Of course, you could join me as a partner. (⁶We share) _____ the profits.

This disco (⁷be) _____ a great success, because there's nothing for teenagers

in this town at the moment. Every businessman in town (⁸wish) _____ he had

thought of it. In six months (⁹we recover) _____ all the money we've

put into it.

    Look, Ned. (¹⁰You not get) _____ another chance like this! The thing is, I

can buy it at a really low price! It's a nightclub at the moment. But the owner has had trouble with the

police, and (¹¹he not be able) _____ to continue with the club much

longer. He wants to get rid of it, so (¹²he sell) _____ it to me cheap. We've

already agreed matters on the telephone, and (¹³I meet) _____ him tomorrow. The

timetable is that (¹⁴we sign) _____ the agreement tomorrow, and (¹⁵I

pay) _____ him the money within fourteen days. I know that if I don't pay in

time, (¹⁶he send) _____ some of his friends round to see me. So I must get

the money, somehow.'

2 Can you find an example in the above verb phrases of the following? Write down the numbers.

1 a promise _____

2 an intention already decided, or firm determination _____

3 a future situation with signs or causes in the present _____

4 a prediction _____

5 something routine, or natural, that will happen as a matter of course _____

6 an arrangement made with another person _____

7 an action belonging to a fixed timetable _____

8 something that will be completed by a certain time in the future _____

3 Write sentences giving your own ideas, or find out what a friend thinks, about:

1 the date of an important development in science (e.g. the first people to land on Mars)

People will land on Mars in _____

2 the next winner of an important sporting event (e.g. the World Football Cup)

_____

3 a future event in your country

_____

4 a promise you have made, or think you **ought** to make to your husband, wife, father, mother, brother, sister, or friend

_____

5 an event which is likely to happen in the future, with signs or causes already visible in the present

_____

6 something natural or routine, which will happen as a matter of course (whether anyone wants it or not)

_____

7 something you'll be doing in one, two three ... (choose a number) years' time

_____

8 something that will have happened by 1995, 2000, 2010 ... (choose a date)

_____

9 an arrangement you have made with another person, or a journey you have planned

_____

10 something which is due to happen as part of your timetable or programme

_____

33 Reported statements

Direct speech
'I want to buy it.'
'I've come to mend the machine.'
'I lost my watch.'
'I'll help with the work.'

Reported speech (no change of tense)

He says (that)	he wants to buy it. he's come to mend the machine. he lost his watch. he'll help with the work.

Notes

Would is used for the 'conditional' form of the verb: *he would help*, etc.
(*would* is the same for all persons).

am/is → was; are → were;
present progressive → past progressive;
won't → wouldn't

Both *had* and *would* occur as *'d* informally.

Reported speech (with change of tense)

He *said* (that)	he want*ed* to buy it. (present → past).
	
	he *had come* to mend the machine.
	    (present perfect → past perfect)
	
	he *had lost* his watch.
	    (past simple → past perfect)
	or
	he *lost* his watch. (no change needed if the time sequence is clear)
	
	he *would help* with the work.
	    (will → would)

1 Pacifica has a new government today. The new president, Mrs Goodman, is making a speech about the old government (of President Badley), and explaining what the new government plans to do.

1 Badley has damaged the country.

2 The country has not been well-governed.

3 Badley's government acted dishonestly.

4 We will form an honest government.

5 Dishonest officials will be punished.

6 We won't prevent anyone from giving his opinion.

7 There won't be any return to the bad old days.

8 I have promised the people this, and I will keep my word.

9 We are going to put the country right.

10 A new age is beginning for everyone.

Not everyone who is listening to the speech agrees with it. Write
sentences as in the example.

1 _She says Badley has damaged the country - but he hasn't._

2 _____

3 _____

4 _____

5 _____

6 _____

_____

7 _____

_____

8 _____

_____

9 _____

10 _____

2 What does the ambassador from Atlantica report back to his
government? Write sentences as in the example.

1 _She said that Badley had damaged the country._

2 _____

3 _____

4 _____

5 _____

6 _____

7 _____

8 _____

_____

9 _____

10 _____

34 Reported questions and answers

For reported questions, tense changes after *He asked, I wondered*, etc. are the same as for reported statements.

'Do they want to buy it?' 'Have you seen my book?' 'Did she do it?' 'Will he arrive in time?'	I asked She wondered He wanted to know *etc.*	if whether	they wanted to buy it. he had seen her book. she had done it. he would arrive in time.
'What do they want to buy?' 'Which book have you seen?' 'Who did it?' 'When will he arrive?'			what they wanted to buy. which book he had seen. who had done it. *or* who did it. when he would arrive.

Note how the word order of questions changes when they become reported questions.

1 After taking part in a big bank robbery, Donald Boggs escaped abroad, to places where the British police couldn't get him. Now he is living in San Bernardo. Ted Slant, a British journalist, has come to interview him. Write reports from the interview as in the example.

1

SLANT: What part did you play in the robbery?
BOGGS: I drove the car for the getaway.

2

SLANT: How long have you been living in San Bernardo?
BOGGS: I've been here for six years. I was living in San Pedro before, but the police there threw me out.

Ted Slant's report

1 I asked him __what part he had played in the robbery__

_____ and he told me _____

_____

_____ for the getaway.

2 I wanted to know _____

_____

_____ . I discovered that

_____

_____ . He _____

_____ in San Pedro before,

but the police there _____

_____ .

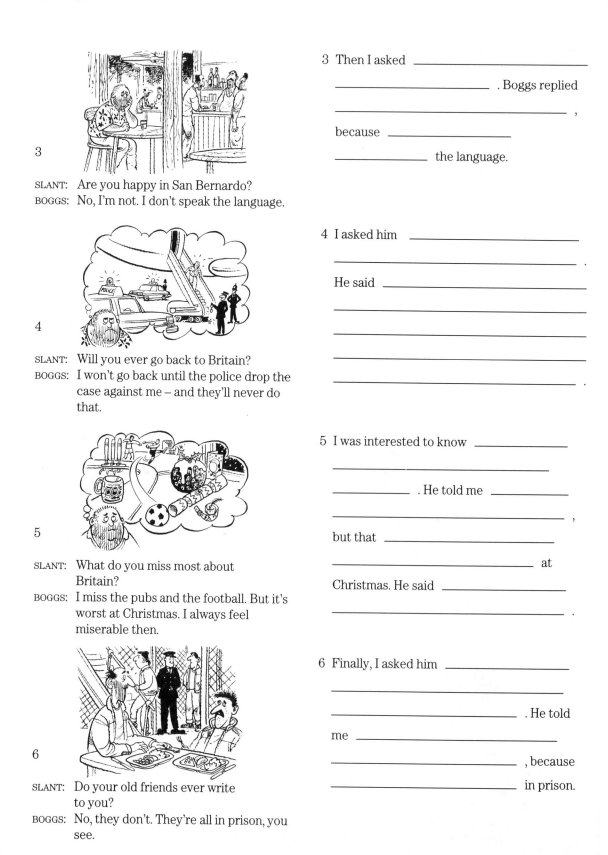

3

SLANT: Are you happy in San Bernardo?
BOGGS: No, I'm not. I don't speak the language.

4

SLANT: Will you ever go back to Britain?
BOGGS: I won't go back until the police drop the case against me – and they'll never do that.

5

SLANT: What do you miss most about Britain?
BOGGS: I miss the pubs and the football. But it's worst at Christmas. I always feel miserable then.

6

SLANT: Do your old friends ever write to you?
BOGGS: No, they don't. They're all in prison, you see.

3 Then I asked _____

_____ . Boggs replied

_____ ,

because _____

_____ the language.

4 I asked him _____

_____ .

He said _____

_____

_____

_____

_____ .

5 I was interested to know _____

_____

_____ . He told me _____

_____ ,

but that _____

_____ at

Christmas. He said _____

_____ .

6 Finally, I asked him _____

_____

_____ . He told

me _____

_____ , because

_____ in prison.

35 Tenses with time clauses

Future		Present or Present perfect
I'll start the work	when	you pay me.
I won't start the work	until	you've paid me.

The present perfect suggests an interval of time between payment and starting the work.

Simple past		Simple past
I started the work	as soon as when after	he paid me.

Simple past		Past perfect
I started the work	after	he had paid me.

The past perfect suggests an interval of time between payment and starting the work.

Present perfect		Simple past
I've lived in Newtown	since	I moved there in 1985.

1 Tom Jones is a gardener at Moxley Hall. He is talking about his life, past and future. Write sentences from the ideas given. Put the time words in brackets at the correct place in the sentence. Change the verbs to a suitable tense.

1 my father (teach) me gardening – I (be) a boy

(*when*) __My father taught me gardening when I was a boy.__

2 the offer of a job at Moxley (come) – I (join) the army

(*after*) But _____

3 I (not start) at Moxley – I (leave) the army

(*until*) So _____

4 I (start) – I (know) I would like it here

(*as soon as*) _____

5 I (be) here – I (start) the job in 1961

(*since*) _____

6 the head gardener (retire) next year – I (become) head gardener in his place

(*when*) _____

7 I (get) a rise in my wages – I (be) head gardener

(*as soon as*) _____

36 *If* with situations which are real possibilities

Present	Future
If you *hurry*,	you *'ll get* there in time.

An *if*-clause of this type is sometimes known as the 'first conditional'.

Present	Present or Future	
If water *is heated* to 100°C.	it *boils.* it *will boil.*	
If a baby *is* hungry,	it usually *starts* it *will* usually *start*	to cry.

An *if*-clause can be used in stating general rules or laws.

1 Ann and Celia are writers for television. They are discussing how to continue a 'soap opera' (a story which goes on week after week). Underline the correct choices in the dialogue below. Sometimes **both** choices are correct. Note that ø = 'no word at all'.

CELIA: The problem is, [1]*if/ø* Margaret [2]*will marry/marries* Henry, [3]*if/ø* our viewers [4]*don't/won't* like it.

ANN: Why not?

CELIA: Well, Henry's so lazy. As I see it, [5]*if/ø* a person [6]*is/will be* energetic, like Margaret, [7]*if/ø* she [8]*isn't/won't be* the right kind of person for someone like Henry.

ANN: Maybe you're right. But often [9]*if/ø* people [10]*are/will be* attracted to each other [11]*if/ø* they [12]*are/will be* different from each other.

CELIA: OK. I've got an idea: [13]*if/ø* people [14]*always get/will always get* interested [15]*if/ø* there [16]*is/will be* some character they really dislike. Right? So let's make Henry really unpleasant. Then [17]*if/ø* it [18]*looks/will look* as if Margaret is going to marry Henry, [19]*if/ø* people [20]*feel/will feel* sorry for her. And of course, [21]*if/ø* everyone [22]*is/will be* happy [23]*if/ø* we [24]*save/'ll save* her from Henry at the last moment.

37 *If* with situations which are unlikely or unreal

An *if* clause of this type is sometimes known as the 'second conditional'.

¹**Past**	**'Would'**
If she *went* to work in France	she ²*would learn* French very quickly.
(these things are unlikely to happen)	
If I ³*were* younger	I *would apply* for the job.
(I am not younger, so these are not real possibilities)	

'Would'	**Past**
They *would be* very angry	if they *found out.*
(these things are unlikely to happen)	
I *would take* his remarks seriously	if I *didn't know* him so well.
(but I know him, so these are not real possibilities.)	

1 With this type of *if*-clause, the 'past' form is usually the simple past, but could also be past progressive: *If you* **were living** *in France, you* **would have to** *go to school there.*
2 *Would* can occur as *'d* informally.
3 Note that *If I/he/she/it* **were**... is still considered more correct than *If I/he/she/it* **was**... in formal writing. But *If I/he/she/it* **was**... is widely used.

1 Millford Football Club isn't doing very well. The manager is dreaming of things that are unlikely to happen, or are not real possibilities. Write down what he thinks, according to the information given below. Decide whether the *if*-clause should go in the first or the second half of the sentence.

1 We pay higher wages.
 If we paid higher wages

We attract better players.
 we would attract better players.

LEAGUE TABLE					
TEAM	Played	Won	Lost	Drew	Pts.
MILLFORD	10	9	0	1	28
LIVERPOOL	11	3	7	1	10

2 More people come and watch us.

We win more matches.

3 We have our team from 1921–22.

We win the cup.

4 We score a lot of goals.

Diego Maradona plays for us.

5 Our goalkeeper doesn't have a broken leg.

He is the best goalkeeper in the league.

6 I am sensible.

I'm not working for this club.

7 Our players run much faster.

They don't smoke.

8 Our striker is taller.

He scores more goals with his head.

38 *If* with situations which were possible in the past, but did not occur

An *if*-clause of this type is sometimes called the 'third conditional'.

Past perfect	**'Would have'**
If I *had seen* her	I *would have* spoken to her.

(but I didn't see her, and I didn't speak to her)

'Would have'	**Past perfect**
She *wouldn't have* succeeded	if she *hadn't worked* hard.

(but she did succeed, and she did work hard)

Would have and *wouldn't have* are the same for all persons:

I **would have** helped her.
She **would have** done it.
They **wouldn't have** known etc.

Would have can occur as *'d have* informally.

1 The Principal of the Express School of English is thinking about his life, and the conditions that led him to do things. What does he say to himself? Write sentences with an *if*-clause.

1 (*I started the school after the bank lent me £50,000.*) If the bank __hadn't lent me__ ___£50,000___ I __wouldn't__ __have started__ the school.

2 (*I continued because the school was a success.*) I _____ _____ if the school _____ a success.

3 (*We won the Pacifica University contract, so we didn't have money problems.*) If we _____ _____ the Pacifica University contract, we _____ _____ money problems.

4 (*I didn't retire, so we didn't go to live in Italy.*) If I _____ we _____ to live in Italy.

5 (*We didn't build another language lab because there weren't enough students.*) We _____ _____ another language lab if _____ enough students.

6 (*We didn't move to a better building because the rent for this building was so low.*) We _____ to a better building if the rent for this building _____ so low.

7 (*Anyway, our teachers stayed with us because there was a friendly atmosphere.*) Anyway, our teachers _____ with us if _____ _____ a friendly atmosphere.

2 Tell your neighbour about events or decisions which made a difference to **your** life. Use *if* with the past perfect tense.

39 Mixed conditional and time clauses

1 Two scouts, Alan and Bob, are sheltering from a storm. They are discussing what has happened, and what to do now. Complete the conversation with a suitable form of the verb in brackets.

ALAN: We ([1]carry on) _____'ll carry on_____ with our walk when the weather ([2]clear up) _____ .

BOB: Yes. But if I ([3]know) _____ the weather was going to be this bad, I ([4]never set out) _____ .

ALAN: Well, it's a bit brighter now. If it ([5]stop) _____ raining, we ([6]easily be) _____ back at the camp by sunset.

BOB: I suppose things could be worse. Do you remember the hill-walk last year? We ([7]have to) _____ turn back almost as soon as we ([8]start) _____ , when Charlie Dickson ([9]break) _____ his ankle.

ALAN: That's right. And that was after we ([10]spend) _____ ages preparing for the walk.

BOB: Still, we were lucky that the accident happened so soon after we ([11]set out) _____ . If it ([12]happen) _____ later, we ([13]have to) _____ carry Charlie for miles.

ALAN: Well just at this moment, I couldn't carry anybody. If a helicopter ([14]come) _____ over the top of that hill, I ([15]wave) _____ to the pilot for a lift.

BOB: There isn't much chance of that. Anyway, my problem is my feet. They're killing me! I ([16]put) _____ some ointment on them if I ([17]have) _____ any. But I forgot to pack it.

ALAN: Me too. But the rain's stopped, so let's go. Just think! When we ([18]get) _____ a good, hot meal at the camp tonight, we ([19]be) _____ glad that we came.

Irregular verbs

(ed) means that the regular form in *ed* is an alternative to the irregular form.

Base	Past simple	Past perfect	Base	Past simple	Past perfect
arise	arose	have arisen	lie	lay	have lain
awake	awoke	have awoken	light	lit/lighted	have lit/lighted
bear*	bore	have borne	lose	lost	have lost
beat	beat	have beaten	make	made	have made
become	became	have become	mean	meant	have meant
begin	began	have begun	meet	met	have met
bend	bent	have bent	pay	paid	have paid
bet	bet	have bet	put	put	have put
bind	bound	have bound	read	read	have read
bite	bit	have bitten	ride	rode	have ridden
bleed	bled	have bled	ring	rang	have rung
blow	blew	have blown	rise	rose	have risen
break	broke	have broken	run	ran	have run
breed	bred	have bred	saw	sawed	have sawn (ed)
bring	brought	have brought	say	said	have said
broadcast	broadcast	have broadcast	see	saw	have seen
build	built	have built	seek	sought	have sought
burn	burnt/burned	have burnt/burned	sell	sold	have sold
burst	burst	have burst	send	sent	have sent
buy	bought	have bought	set	set	have set
cast	cast	have cast	sew	sewed	have sewn (ed)
catch	caught	have caught	shake	shook	have shaken
choose	chose	have chosen	shine	shone	have shone
cling	clung	have clung	shoot	shot	have shot
come	came	have come	show	showed	have shown
cost	cost	have cost	shrink	shrank	have shrunk
creep	crept	have crept	shut	shut	have shut
cut	cut	have cut	sing	sang	have sung
deal	dealt	have dealt	sink	sank	have sunk
dig	dug	have dug	sit	sat	have sat
do	did	have done	sleep	slept	have slept
draw	drew	have drawn	smell	smelt/smelled	have smelt/smelled
dream	dreamt/dreamed	have dreamt/dreamed	sow	sowed	have sown/sowed
drink	drank	have drunk	speak	spoke	have spoken
drive	drive	have driven	speed	sped	have sped
eat	ate	have eaten	spend	spent	have spent
fall	fell	have fallen	spin	spun	have spun
feed	fed	have fed	spit	spat	have spat
feel	felt	have felt	split	split	have split
fight	fought	have fought	spoil	spoilt/spoiled	have spoilt/spoiled
find	found	have found	spread	spread	have spread
flee	fled	have fled	spring	sprang	have sprung
fly	flew	have flown	stand	stood	have stood
forbid	forbade	have forbidden	steal	stole	have stolen
forecast	forecast	have forecast	stick	stuck	have stuck
forget	forgot	have forgotten	sting	stung	have stung
forgive	forgave	have forgiven	stink	stank	have stunk
freeze	froze	have frozen	strike	struck	have struck
get	got	have got	swear	swore	have sworn
give	gave	have given	sweep	swept	have swept
go	went	have gone	swim	swam	have swum
grow	grew	have grown	swing	swung	have swung
hang	hung	have hung	take	took	have taken
hear	heard	have heard	teach	taught	have taught
hide	hid	have hid/hidden	tear	tore	have torn
hit	hit	have hit	tell	told	have told
hold	held	have held	think	thought	have thought
hurt	hurt	have hurt	throw	threw	have thrown
keep	kept	have kept	thrust	thrust	have thrust
kneel	knelt/kneeled	have knelt/kneeled	understand	understood	have understood
knit	knit	have knit (ted)	wake	woke	have woken
know	knew	have known	wear	wore	have worn
lay	laid	have laid	weep	wept	have wept
lead	led	have led	win	won	have won
lean	leant/leaned	have leant/leaned	wind	wound	have wound
leap	leapt/leaped	have leapt/leaped	withdraw	withdrew	have withdrawn
learn	learnt/learned	have learnt/learned	write	wrote	have written
leave	left	have left			
lend	lent	have lent			
let	let	have let			

*bear is often used in the passive, with a different past participle, e.g. *I was born in 1980.*

Answer key

1 Simple present (pages 4–5)

1 1 begin 2 say 3 flies 4 grows
5 joins 6 goes 7 put 8 comes
9 chooses 10 turn 11 covers
12 tell 13 applauds 14 throw
15 catches 16 disappear 17 tries
18 weighs 19 clap 20 rises
21 finishes 22 flashes 23 plays
24 hides 25 vanish

2 1 How does the bird fly out of the
cage? 2 How does Henri escape
from the box? 3 How do the balls
disappear? 4 How does the piano
rise into the air? 5 How do you do
the trick with the cards? 6 How do
you make the grey mist? 7 How do
you and Henri vanish at the end?
8 How long does your act last?

2 Simple present (pages 6–7)

1 1 Abdullah doesn't do all the written
work. 2 Why doesn't he do it?
3 Because he only needs spoken
English in his job. 4 I don't use the
computer with my group. 5 Why
don't you use it? 6 Because the
programmes for it don't seem very
useful. 7 Lucia and Leif don't find
the work interesting. 8 Why don't
they find it interesting? 9 They
think the level is too low for them.
10 Gustav and I don't get on well.
11 Oh? Why don't you get on?
12 The problem is, we don't share the
same political opinions. 13 Fatma
doesn't come to the class before lunch
on Friday mornings. 14 Why doesn't
she come? 15 Because she goes to
the mosque then. 16 The reading
textbook doesn't suit the students in
my group. 17 Why doesn't it suit
them? 18 It doesn't give them the
kind of practice they need. 19 Julio
and Sergio don't like each other.
20 Why don't they like each other?
21 Oh, it's because they disagree
about almost everything.

2 1 hate 2 do you want 3 don't we
go 4 shows 5 don't feel 6 says
7 know 8 like 9 don't we go
10 doesn't appeal 11 don't you go
12 doesn't mater 13 stay 14 like
15 lives 16 stays 17 don't go
18 doesn't get out

3 *Example*
A: Why don't we go swimming?
It's a nice day.
B: No, I don't want to go swimming
today. I've got a bad cold. etc.

3 Present progressive (pages 8–9)

1 1 isn't typing ... She's dancing
2 's sleeping ... He isn't standing
3 aren't repairing ... They're listening
4 's sitting ... It isn't catching
5 isn't answering ... She's letting
6 isn't printing ... It's getting
7 're cutting ... They aren't making
8 'm not eating ... I'm trying

4 Present progressive (pages 10–11)

1 1 are you standing 2 aren't you
helping 3 aren't doing 4 Susie's
doing 5 is Terry taking 6 isn't he
taking 7 He's taking 8 They're
using 8 Aren't you frying 10 are
they burning/aren't they burning
11 I'm making 12 am I doing
13 am I not lying/aren't I lying
14 You're helping

5 Mixed present simple and progressive forms (pages 12–13)

1 1 do you come from 2 no change
3 I don't live 4 no change 5 Don't
they make/Do they make 6 is paying
7 My company doesn't send 8 I'm
paying 9 are you taking 10 I'm
not doing 11 I'm trying 12 there
doesn't seem 13 I'm improving
14 do you know 15 the school is
organising 16 I don't know 17 no
change 18 don't we meet

2 1 you're doing 2 makes 3 I read
4 you see 5 are dying 6 makes
7 Doesn't it make 8 feel 9 do you
say 10 helps 11 are living
12 don't want 13 are suffering
14 don't see 15 I'm saying
16 don't need 17 do I look 18 I
help

6 Simple past (pages 14–15)

1 (Report 1)
1 swam 2 fell 3 caught
4 brought 5 revived
(Report 2)
6 won 7 taught 8 found
9 thrust 10 blew 11 held on
12 shot 13 went on
(Report 3)
14 stopped 15 discovered
16 learned 17 saw 18 said
19 had 20 put 21 drove
22 thought
(Report 4)
23 struck 24 started
25 destroyed 26 caused 27 took

2 1 How far did she swim? 2 Where
did she bring him? 3 How did she
revive him? 4 How long did they
hold on? 5 When did he learn to
drive? 6 Where did he see the car?
7 What did it strike? 8 How much
damage did it cause? 9 How long did
it take (them)?

7 Simple past (page 16)

1 ANN: The plane didn't leave until
11.30 – four hours late.
DICK: Didn't they say why it was late?
ANN: No, they didn't. And then
someone was supposed to meet
us. But he didn't arrive. Or
perhaps he'd come earlier and
gone away again.
DICK: Perhaps he didn't know about
the plane being late.
ANN: Maybe. Anyway, when we finally
got to the hotel, the hotel didn't
want to give us rooms. They
didn't have a record of our
reservation.
DICK: Didn't the travel company send
the hotel a list of names?
ANN: Apparently not. Still they let us
stay in the end.
DICK: From what you say, it sounds as
if your holiday didn't go very
well.
ANN: Well, a lot of things happened
that I didn't expect.

8 Simple past (page 17)

1 1 no change 2 The mist didn't
cover 3 didn't you get back 4 no
change 5 You didn't have to 6 we
didn't take 7 You didn't take
8 didn't you check 9 no change
10 no change 11 didn't you have
12 no change 13 Didn't you take
14 no change 15 he didn't know
16 no change

9 Past progressive (pages 18–19)

1 1 the girl was trying 2 she wasn't
trying 3 They were riding 4 he
was chasing 5 were they doing
6 Were they climbing 7 Weren't
they climbing 8 were making
9 was working 10 He wasn't
working 11 He was planning
12 wasn't he aiming 13 He was
shooting 14 He was hoping 15 I
wasn't watching 16 weren't you
watching 17 you weren't watching
18 you were snoring

10 Past progressive and simple past (pages 20–21)

1 1 While Dell fans were entering the
ground, a group of Lee fans arrived.
2 Several of our men received injuries
while we were trying to keep the
groups of fans apart. 3 We held/
were holding our ground well until a
group of Dell fans broke through our

lines.   4 When the two groups met, violent fighting broke out. (no past continuous with either verb)
5 While I was attempting to arrest one hooligan a brick struck me on the head.   6 Several shopkeepers complained to us because the fans were causing/the fans caused a lot of damage.   7 While all this was going on outside, fans were throwing/fans threw stones inside the ground.
8 The situation was becoming/The situation became serious, so we radioed for extra men.   9 However, while we were waiting/we waited for extra men the situation became calm.

11 Present perfect (pages 22–23)

1 1 Marie, have you ever ridden a horse?
Me? Oh no, I've never ridden a horse.
2 Pierre, have you ever ridden a horse?
Yes, I've ridden a horse a few times.
3 Pierre, has Marie ever sung in public?
Yes, she's often sung in public.
4 Marie, have you ever wanted to live in America?
No, I've never wanted to live in America.
5 Marie, has Pierre ever wanted to live in America?
Yes, he's always wanted to live in America.
6 Monsieur Leblanc, have Pierre and Marie ever forgotten your birthday?
Yes, they've forgotten my birthday once or twice.
7 Marie, have you ever been to England?
Yes, I've been to England.
8 Marie, have we ever met before/have I ever met you before?
Yes, we've met several times/you've met me several times.
9 Have I ever met Pierre before?
No, you've never met before/you've never met him before.

12 Present perfect (page 24)

1 1 Sid hasn't smoked for 18 years.   2 Don has been a vegetarian since 1980.   3 Liza has been interested in healthy eating for five years.   4 Sam hasn't drunk alcohol since his car accident.   5 I've run two kilometres every morning since 1985.   6 Mary hasn't stayed up after midnight for two years.
7 Sue and Pam haven't taken useless medicines since they

joined the club.   8 Bob and I have played squash every Friday night since the squash court opened

13 Present perfect (page 25)

1 1 hasn't it arrived   2 no change   3 they haven't had   4 Haven't I told   5 no change   6 I haven't had   7 The cleaner hasn't emptied   8 no change   9 she hasn't told   10 no change   11 haven't you forgotten   12 no change   13 you haven't put   14 no change

14 Present perfect progressive (page 26)

1 1 I've been looking   2 someone has been using   3 Have you been doing   4 I haven't been using   5 I've been eating   6 Have they been entertaining   7 Vera has been discussing   8 she hasn't been cooking   9 she's been staying   10 we've been spending   11 Prices have been going up

15 Present perfect (page 27)

1 1 It has been   2 We have/'ve been hoping   3 haven't you written/have you not written   4 have always meant   5 I have/'ve sent   6 has been saving   7 we have/'ve put   8 has gone on   9 has not/hasn't been enjoying (or enjoyed)   10 has had to   11 He has/'s had   12 has been coming   13 we have/'ve managed   14 Have you seen   15 he has/'s left   16 We have/'ve been getting   17 He has not/hasn't said   18 he has/he's met   19 you have/'ve done

16 Present perfect and simple past (page 28)

1 1 began   2 continued   3 were   4 took place   5 have staged   6 have staged   7 became   8 was   9 have taken part,   10 has equalled   11 won   12 have seen   13 collapsed   14 came   15 helped   16 broke   17 participated   18 have grown   19 have gone

17 Past perfect (page 29)

1 1 I had climbed a mountain.
2 The rope hadn't broken.   3 My girlfriend had agreed to marry me.
4 A letter had come with good news about my exams.   5 I had spent a wonderful holiday in Wales.   6 My favourite team had won the football championship.

2 1 What had you done?   2 What hadn't broken?   3 What had she

agreed to do?   4 What had the letter come with?   5 Where had you spent a wonderful holiday?   6 What had it won?

18 Past perfect progressive (page 31)

1 1 had been working   2 had been giving away   3 had not been cooperating   4 had been having   5 had been listening   6 had not been receiving   7 had not been getting   8 had been feeding   9 had been sending   10 had not been carrying out

19 Past perfect (page 32)

1 1 no change   2 Hadn't you tried it on   3 no change   4 I hadn't tried on   5 I'd been making   6 no change   7 no change   8 Had he been celebrating   9 He'd been having   10 he hadn't slept   11 no change   12 He'd been talking   13 Had his father given/been giving   14 no change

20 Mixed past and perfect forms (page 33)

1 1 has become   2 began   3 was studying   4 stood   5 did not win   6 had ever been   7 elected/had elected/had been electing   8 just laughed   9 got up   10 has shown   11 has never been   12 has fought/been fighting   13 were continually writing/continually wrote   14 treated/were treating/had treated   15 had thrown them out/threw them out   16 always took/had/has always taken   17 interviewed   18 was planning   19 has/had already persuaded   20 told

21 Mixed past and perfect forms (page 34)

1 (These are examples only; many different answers are possible.)
1 I was watching television at the time.   2 Why haven't you done your homework?   3 Didn't you come to the meeting?/Weren't you at the meeting?   4 The reason was that my car broke down on the way.   5 I'm sorry that you've been ill/haven't been well recently.   6 I had been writing on the wall of my bedroom/making a noise in the classroom.   7 I think it was because Arctica had taken some land from Pacifica/had helped Pacifica's enemies.   8 Did you expect to pass (it)?   9 Was she driving at the time?/ Who was driving the car?

22 Future with *will* and *shall* (page 35)

1 Promises
1 will 2 'll 3 'll 4 won't 5 'll
6 won't 7 'll 8 'll 9 'll 10 will
11 won't 12 won't 13 'll
14 won't 15 won't 16 'll 17 'll

2 Predictions
These are examples only; students make their own predictions.)
1 I think they'll be powered by electric batteries. They won't be powered by atomic power (in my opinion). 2 People will still smoke cigarettes (but they won't smoke as many cigarettes as they smoke now).
3 In my opinion, they won't speak the same language all over the world (but they will speak fewer languages than they speak now). 4 There won't be drugs against every kind of disease (but there will be a lot of new drugs).
5 For example: There will be more aeroplanes/There won't be as many diseases/The world will be warmer/The deserts will get bigger, etc.
6 and 7 For example: I'll have a different job/I'll be married/I won't be rich, etc.

23 Questions with *shall* for offers, suggestions, and requests (page 37)

1 1 Shall I do the shopping? 2 Shall we go to Spain for our holiday this year? 3 Shall we dance? 4 Where shall we take Aunt Martha when she comes to visit? 5 Shall I cook a meal for you? 6 What shall I do if the money doesn't reach me in time?
7 What shall I wear at the wedding?

24 Future with *will* and *shall* (page 38)

11 1 no change 2 they won't attack
3 no change 4 Will they be
5 they won't be 6 will there be
7 there won't be 8 no change
9 Shall I go up 10 will you let
11 no change 12 no change
13 They won't see 14 we won't let
15 Shall we do 16 We won't give
17 no change

25 Future with *going to* (pages 39–41)

1 Situation with signs observable in present (page 39)
(Answers, especially the reasons, may vary)
1 Are the monkeys going to reach the bananas?
Yes, they're going to reach the bananas. One monkey can climb onto the other monkey.

No, they aren't going to reach the bananas. The stick is too short/the bananas are too high.
2 Are they going to find the treasure?
Yes, they are going to find the treasure. They can use a helicopter/climb over the walls, etc.
No, they aren't going to find the treasure. There's no way to it/Every path is blocked, etc.
3. Is she going to rescue the man in the water?
Yes, she's going to rescue the man in the water. She has a long rope.
No, she isn't going to rescue the man in the water. The rope is going to break.
4 Is the building going to fall down?
Yes, it's going to fall down. It's leaning over/leaning to one side./It isn't straight, etc.
No, it isn't going to fall down. It has been like this for a long time.
5 Is it going to get dark?
Yes, it's going to get dark. The sun is setting/going down.
No, it isn't going to get dark. The sun is rising.
6 Is she going to get married?
Yes, she's going to get married. She's wearing a wedding dress.
No, she isn't going to get married. She's in a play/acting in a play/singing in an opera, etc.

2 Intentions already decided and firm determination (page 41)
1 I'm going to buy a new dress.
2 What kind of dress are you going to buy? 3 It's going to be an evening dress. 4 You're not going to/You aren't going to play football in the playground, do you hear? 5 I'm going to find/catch the boy who wrote this message! I'm not going to let him get away with it! 6 Soldiers! The time has come! Tomorrow we/you are going to march into Pacifica! 7 The people of Pacifica are our brothers. We're not going to/aren't going to fight them!

26 Mixed *will/shall* and *going to* forms (page 42)

1 1 It's going to be 2 Shall we go
3 I'll go 4 I'm not going to swim/I won't (or shan't) swim 5 I'll swim
6 I'm going to take/I'll take 7 I'll be glad 8 I'm going to lie 9 it'll do or it's going to do (possible, but less likely) 10 there's going to be/there'll be 11 there won't be
12 We'll probably have 13 shall we do/are we going to do 14 Shall I make 15 I'll make

2 Both *will/shall* and going to can be used in 4, 6, 9, 10, 13.

27 Future expressed by present progressive (page 43)

1 1 *a* 2 *a* 3 *b* 4 *c* 5 *a*

28 Future expressed by simple present (page 44)

1 1 assemble 2 give 3 makes
4 divide 5 're going to try out
6 meet 7 arrives 8 is going to get
9 visit 10 returns 11 begins
12 have 13 is going to enjoy
14 finishes

29 Future progressive with *will + ing* (page 45)

1 1 will Sue be doing 2 Will she be going 3 She'll be playing 4 She won't be riding 5 they'll be camping
6 They'll be camping 7 They won't be camping 8 Will you be having
9 We'll be staying 10 We won't be gazing 11 You'll be coming 12 I'll be making 13 I won't/shan't be making 14 he'll be having 15 He'll be eating 16 He won't be eating
17 Will she be staying 18 she won't be coming back

30 Future progressive contrasted with *will* future, etc. (page 47)

1 1 *c* 2 *c* 3 *c* 4 *b* 5 *a* 6 *b*
7 *b* 8 *c* 9 *c* 10 *b*

31 Future perfect contrasted with future progressive (page 48)

1 1 will have risen ... will not have risen 2 will be marvelling ... will not have equalled 3 shall have overtaken 4 will be producing
5 will have doubled 6 we shall have built 7 you will be enjoying

32 Mixed forms expressing the future (pages 49–50)

1 1 I'm going to open 2 it'll take/it's going to take 3 Will you lend 4 I'll pay 5 you won't have to 6 We'll share 7 will be/is going to be
8 will wish/will be wishing/is going to wish 9 we'll have recovered
10 You won't get/You're not going to get 11 he won't be able 12 he's selling/he'll sell/he's going to sell
13 I'm meeting/I'm going to meet
14 we sign/we're going to sign/we'll sign 15 I pay/I'm going to pay
16 he'll send/he's going to send/he'll be sending